WELBECK
CHILDREN'S BOOKS

First published in Great Britain in 2026 by Welbeck Children's Books
An imprint of Hachette Children's Group

ISBN: 978 1 80453 935 4

All rights reserved. This book is sold subject to the condition that it may not be reproduced, stored in a retrieval system, or transmitted in any form or by any means, electronic, mechanical, photocopying, recording, or otherwise, without the publisher's prior consent.

Writer: Hannah Dolan
Illustrator: Carl Pearce

Printed in the UK
10 9 8 7 6 5 4 3 2 1

Statistics and records correct as of December 2025

All names, characters, trademarks, service marks, and trade names referred to herein are the property of their respective owners and are used solely for identification purposes. This book is a publication of Welbeck Children's Books and has not been licensed, approved, sponsored, or endorsed by any person or entity.

A CIP catalogue record for this book is available from the British Library.

Welbeck Children's Books
An imprint of Hachette Children's Group
Part of Hodder & Stoughton Limited
Carmelite House, 50 Victoria Embankment
London EC4Y 0DZ

An Hachette UK Company
www.hachette.co.uk
www.hachettechildrens.co.uk

The authorised representative in the EEA
is Hachette Ireland, 8 Castlecourt Centre,
Dublin 15, D15 XTP3, Ireland
(email: info@hbgi.ie)

BASKETBALL SUPERSTARS

KEVIN DURANT

HANNAH DOLAN
CARL PEARCE

CONTENTS

CHAPTER 1 **SCORING SUPERSTAR** 5

CHAPTER 2 **LITTLE KEVIN** 13

CHAPTER 3 **TEENAGE STAR** 27

CHAPTER 4 **ONE AND DONE** 43

CHAPTER 5 **NBA GIANT** 59

CHAPTER 6 **CHASING GREATNESS** 71

CHAPTER 7 **NUMBER ONE** 93

CHAPTER 8 **GOING FOR GOLD** 107

CHAPTER 9 **OFF THE COURT** 119

CHAPTER 10 **BASKETBALL TERMS** 127

CHAPTER 1
SCORING SUPERSTAR

HUMBLE HERO

Kevin Durant is one of the most skilled players ever to set foot on a basketball court.

NBA franchises build teams around his talents, and KD always delivers. He has brought enormous success and big scores to every team he's ever played for.

Before Kevin came along, no player of his height had ever been able to handle the ball or shoot as efficiently as Kevin can. His uniqueness has changed the game – and now everyone wants to find a player like him!

Today, Kevin stands tall as one of the highest scorers in NBA history, and he just keeps on going! As he enters his eighteenth NBA season, Kevin is defying the odds and still playing basketball at the highest level.

Along the way, Kevin has always stayed humble, grounded and grateful to those who have helped him get to where he is.

This is the story of how he transformed from a lanky, insecure kid to one of the basketball greats.

WHAT MAKES KEVIN SO AWESOME?

SHOOTING

Kevin makes shooting from anywhere on the court look like a piece of cake!

HEIGHT

At 6 ft 11 in (2.11m) tall – even 7 ft in basketball shoes! – Kevin can shoot over other players' heads.

BALL-HANDLING

KD's ball control and dribbling skills help him quickly make space on the court.

ACCURACY

When Kevin takes a shot, he usually makes it accurately – he doesn't like to shoot and miss.

MOVEMENT

Kevin can move very quickly for such a tall player, making him a nightmare to defend against.

LEADERSHIP

Kevin is a natural leader who loves to help his teammates play their best, too.

WORK ETHIC

He is already one of basketball's greats, but Kevin has never stopped working hard to improve his game.

The stats don't lie. Kevin's exceptional NBA career is right there in numbers.

4 NBA Finals performances

2 times NBA champion

2 back-to-back NBA Finals MVP trophies

4 times NBA scoring champion

More than **30,000** career points (and counting)

2 NBA All-star MVPs

4 Olympic gold medals

More than any other male player

15 All-Star Game selections

1 NBA MVP

11 All-NBA team selections

518 career points for Team USA (the most ever)

More than **$300** million fortune

BASKETBALL I.D.

NAME:
Kevin Wayne Durant

DATE OF BIRTH:
29th September, 1988

HOMETOWN:
Washington, D.C.

NATIONALITY: American

HEIGHT: 6ft 11in (2.11m)

POSITION: Power forward / small forward

TEAMS: Seattle SuperSonics/Oklahoma City Thunder, Golden State Warriors, Brooklyn Nets, Phoenix Suns, Houston Rockets

JERSEY NUMBER: 35, 7

NICKNAMES: KD, Slim Reaper, Durantula, Easy Money Sniper

On 29th September 1988, in District of Columbia Hospital, Washington, D.C., Kevin Durant came into the world.

Kevin was the second child of his parents, Wanda Durant and Wayne Pratt. They already had a son, Tony, who was born almost three years before Kevin.

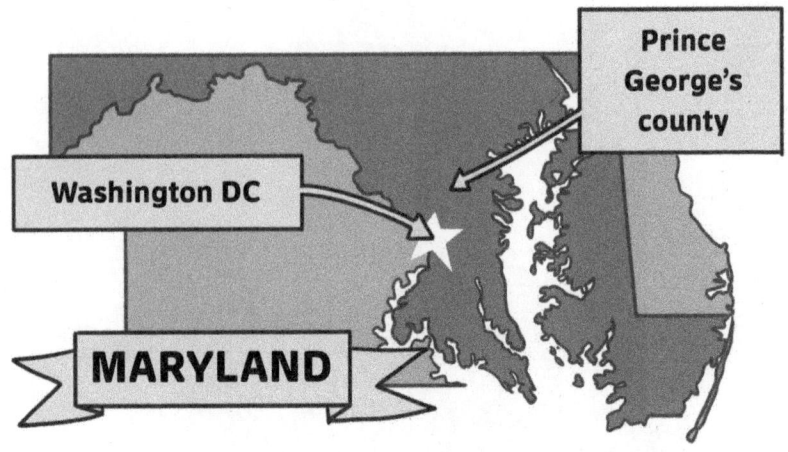

The family lived in Prince George's County, Maryland, an area on the outskirts of Washington, D.C.

Prince George's County is a region famous for producing pro basketball players, including 25 NBA players since 2000. Kevin made a documentary about the stars and their community called *Basketball County: In the Water*.

Wanda was 18 when she had Tony, and she was 21 when Kevin came along. Wayne was very young, too.

When Kevin was only one year old, Kevin's dad Wayne left the family. His mum Wanda started to raise Kevin and his brother Tony alone. This is why Kevin uses his mother's surname, Durant, instead of Pratt.

Life was difficult for Wanda and her two sons because they didn't have much money and they didn't have a permanent place to live. They moved around a lot and had very few possessions.

Wanda worked extremely hard at the post office. She did a night shift when little Kevin and Tony were asleep.

While Wanda was at work, Kevin's grandmother, Barbara, looked after the children. Kevin's Aunt Pearl, his grandmother's sister, cared for them too.

Barbara and Pearl shared a house in Kevin's neighbourhood. They made peanut butter and jelly sandwiches for Kevin and his brother Tony after school and watched cartoons with them. Barbara and Pearl were a constant presence in Kevin's life while his mum worked hard to earn money, and they taught Kevin from a young age just how important family is.

When Kevin was eight, his mum signed him and Tony up to a local gym, Seat Pleasant Activity Centre. She sent the boys there on Saturday mornings to play sports while she was working or running errands.

Kevin started playing basketball at the gym and immediately felt happy and at home there. A coach called Charles Craig, who everyone knew as "Chucky", noticed how good Kevin was and asked him to try out for the gym's basketball team, the PG Jaguars.

Kevin made the team and Chucky gave him jersey number 24. From that point on, Chucky became Kevin's mentor. He taught Kevin all about the game of basketball and how to be the best person he could be.

Chucky loved children. He'd take kids to the movies in his van or give them money for snacks. He'd often take hungry kids at the gym home to his mum for a good meal. Little Kevin was one of them.

The gym became Kevin's second home, and Chucky was like a father figure to him at a time when Kevin didn't have one.

Kevin shone for the PG Jaguars, who played in the AAU (Amateur Athletic Union). People even questioned if Kevin should have worn jersey number 23 instead of 24 because he was the Michael Jordan of the team! Kevin began to dream of making it as a pro basketball player and playing for the NBA one day.

Kevin's mum, Wanda, advised him that he'd have to put in a lot of hard work to make his dream happen, and he listened. He played for hours and hours every day and started running to the gym from his grandmother's house to build up his fitness.

Kevin's Aunt Pearl still played a huge role in his life. Kevin was quiet and didn't have many friends, but he loved talking to Aunt Pearl. He shared his basketball successes with her and she supported him in everything he did. But Aunt Pearl started to miss more and more of his basketball games. When Kevin was just 11 years old, he found out why: Aunt Pearl had lung cancer.

Sadly, the evening Kevin found out about Aunt Pearl's illness was the evening she died. Kevin was by her bedside. Aunt Pearl was a huge loss to Kevin and the whole family.

Kevin continued to spend a lot of his time at the gym, which he called "the rec", and he grew close to another PG Jaguars coach: Taras Brown. Taras saw big potential in little Kevin but he thought Kevin was playing too timidly. He wanted to see Kevin take the ball and try to make more shots. Kevin was reluctant because he didn't want his teammates to think he was hogging the ball.

Taras and Chucky often took Kevin to their homes to watch NBA games. Kevin loved watching Antoine Walker, a power forward for the Boston Celtics, shimmy his shoulders after taking shots. Kevin thought he'd try it before making shots to loosen up his shoulders and calm himself down. It worked, and he still does it today! After games, Kevin would sometimes sleep over on the couch.

Outside of the rec, life wasn't so fun for Kevin. By age 14, he was 6 ft 2 in (1.88 m) – much taller than the other kids in his class – and he was self-conscious about it. Some of the other kids teased him and asked him why he was so tall. Kevin hung his head and wished he could hide away, but he couldn't.

Kevin's mum asked his teachers to put him at the end of the line at school so he didn't stand out so much. She also reassured him that his height was a blessing. His grandma told him that one day he'd love being tall, too, but it was hard for Kevin to think that way when he was being bullied.

But when things got tough at school or in his neighbourhood, Kevin had the rec as a safe haven to literally run to. He knew his friends and coaches there would look out for him, and they would continue to for many years to come.

Taras Brown became another father figure for Kevin, and Kevin started to call him "Godfather". Kevin is still very close to Taras today.

CHAPTER 3
TEENAGE STAR

While playing for the PG Jaguars, Kevin became friends with another neighbourhood kid with a difficult background: Michael Beasley. Michael was also raised by just his mum without much money. In fact, when Michael first joined the team, he stole a box of pizza because he didn't know when he would next eat!

Kevin and Michael became best friends. Michael's mum would drop him off at Kevin's house before school and they'd eat breakfast together before catching the bus to school. They'd then practise and play in the same games after school.

Together, Kevin and Michael made magic for the PG Jaguars! The team beat AAU teams from across the country and won two national championships.

Like Kevin, Michael went on to play in the NBA and they're still friends to this day.

BASKETBALL I.D.

NAME: Michael Beasley
DATE OF BIRTH: 9th January 1989
POSITION: Power forward
TEAMS: Miami Heat, Minnesota Timberwolves, Phoenix Suns, Houston Rockets, Milwaukee Bucks, New York Knicks, Los Angeles Lakers
YEARS IN THE NBA: 2008–2019
RELATIONSHIP TO KEVIN: Childhood friend

People were starting to take notice of Kevin, but he still hadn't reached star potential. When he was 14, Kevin went to play for a better AAU side, the DC Blue Devils.

Around the same time, Kevin started at National Christian Academy high school and immediately made an impact on the school's basketball team, the Eagles. In the first half of his freshman year, he played for the junior varsity squad. By the end of the year, he was on the varsity squad – the best team in the whole school! It was a massive accomplishment for a freshman.

It was also at this time that Kevin's dad, Wayne, came back into Kevin's life. Wayne realised that his two sons needed him, but mending their relationship didn't always go smoothly and it took many years to get back on track.

Kevin's dad

Wayne started coming to some of Kevin's basketball games and hanging out with him. Kevin loved having his dad around. He also got to know his two younger half siblings, Brianna and Rayvonne, who were born while Wayne was away from Kevin's life.

By the end of Kevin's freshman year in high school, he had grown to 6 ft 7 in (2.01m), and now everyone was taking notice. The DC Blue Devils coach, Rob Jackson, promoted Kevin to the A team that travelled the country for games – a team that also featured future NBA star Ty Lawson.

BASKETBALL I.D.

NAME: Ty Lawson

DATE OF BIRTH: 3rd November 1987

POSITION: Point guard

TEAMS: Denver Nuggets, Houston Rockets, Indiana Pacers, Sacramento Kings, Washington Wizards

YEARS IN NBA: 2009–2018

RELATIONSHIP TO KEVIN: Teenage teammate

Both Kevin's coaches in the Blue Devils and at high school were amazed by Kevin's passion and work ethic. When he wasn't playing in games, he was practising for them. With the adopted family he'd created at the gym and all the support and encouragement he had at home, Kevin's life was built around basketball – and it showed.

Everyone wanted to catch a glimpse of Kevin Durant's talents in his sophomore year at high school. Crowds gathered at National Christian Academy's small gym to see him play. He led the school in points scored, and played a big role in the Eagles' wins that season.

That year, the Eagles played in a big tournament called War on the Shore. Lots of college coaches and scouts were there to look out for talented players to get on their rosters. One of those coaches was Russell Springmann from the University of Texas, and he liked what he saw in Kevin.

Russell Springmann

Right after the tournament, Russell called Kevin's high school coach, Rob Brown, and told him he was interested in signing up Kevin to his college team. But that lifechanging offer would have to wait for a few more years... Kevin still had two more years of high school to finish!

While Kevin was riding high at high school, tragedy was about to hit one of the most important people in his life. On 30th April 2005, Kevin's coach and father figure Chucky Craig was shot and killed after breaking up a fight in the street.

Kevin, who was only 16 at the time, was devastated. He wanted to do something to pay tribute to Chucky for the love, support and opportunities he had given him. From that day on, he changed his jersey number from 24 to 35 – the age Chucky was when he died.

Kevin channelled his grief and anger over Chucky's death into action on the basketball court. Chucky always said he wanted to be there when Kevin was drafted to the NBA. That wasn't to be, but Kevin knew he could still do his first mentor proud by making it as a pro with his special number on his jersey.

For his junior year at high school, Kevin moved to Oak Hill Academy, which had one of the greatest basketball teams in the country. The high school was in Mouth of Wilson, Virginia, hundreds of miles and six hours' drive from Kevin's Maryland home, but Kevin wasn't alone – he joined the school alongside his friends Michael Beasley and Ty Lawson.

Many big NBA stars went to Oak Hill Academy, including Ron Mercer, Jerry Stackhouse and Carmelo Anthony. The Oak Hill Warriors have been National High School Champions nine times.

Kevin's junior year at Oak Hill Academy couldn't have gone better. He led the Warriors to a phenomenal record of 32 wins and only one loss!

He sometimes held back on his time with the ball to let other players shine, just like he did back in AAU games with Taras Brown and Chucky as his coaches, but when it really mattered, Kevin knew how to kick into overdrive and bring home the points to win matches.

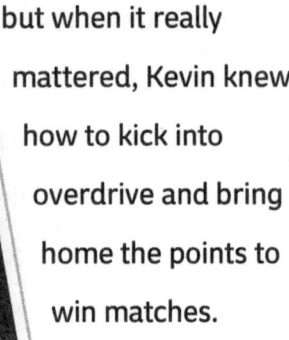

Kevin finished up the season as the team's leading scorer with an average of 19.8 points and 8.8 rebounds. (A rebound is when a player grabs the ball after a missed shot.)

The following year, Kevin was on the move again, this time to Montrose Christian School in Rockville, Maryland. It was a lot closer to home but being nearer his family wasn't the only reason Kevin wanted to go there – he also wanted to be pushed even more towards greatness.

It would have been easy for Kevin to stay at Oak Hill Academy for another year because he was established there, but he wanted to be challenged. He knew that the coach at Montrose Christian was Coach Stu Vetter, one of the best high school coaches in the US – and also one of the toughest.

Stu Vetter

Kevin rose to the challenge! He immediately clicked with the team, which included future NBA star Greivis Vasquez, and he trained, played and studied hard.

By the end of the year, Kevin had upped his points average to 23.6 points and 10.2 rebounds per game. He led the Montrose Christian team to a 20-2 record that season, and they were ranked as the Number 1 high school team by USA Today. They also beat Kevin's old team Oak Hill in a dramatic, end-of-season face-off with his friends Michael Beasley and Ty Lawson!

This was also the year that Taishi Ito came into Kevin's life. Taishi had transferred to Montrose Christian School from Japan and lived with a local woman he called "Grandma".

Taishi and Kevin became good friends and eventually Kevin moved into Grandma's house, too, because he had a long journey to the school from his mum's house. Taishi had to work hard and be very disciplined to play basketball at such a high level, and he influenced Kevin to do the same. They would get up at 5:30am to train before anyone else. When they weren't playing basketball, they helped each other with their studies, listened to hip-hop, and talked long into the night.

Hanging out with Taishi had such a big influence on Kevin in both his life and his career that he later put Taishi's initials, "TI", on the sole of the first shoe he designed for Nike, the KD1.

At the end of his year at Montrose Christian, it was time for Kevin to say goodbye to Taishi and high school basketball. College was calling, and Kevin knew exactly where he was headed.

Taishi Ito was never drafted to the NBA, but he did go on to have a professional basketball career in Japan, playing for Shiga Lakestars.

CHAPTER 4
ONE AND DONE

Before Kevin moved to Montrose Christian School for his senior year, Kevin had already decided where he was going to college: the University of Texas.

Remember the assistant coach at Texas, Russell Springmann? He had spotted Kevin at the War on the Shore tournament back when Kevin was just a high school sophomore. Well, Kevin remembered Russell's interest in him and visited the campus before his senior year. He visited other colleges too, but he liked everything he saw at Texas, including the coaching style of head coach Rick Barnes, who let players be themselves. Kevin was going to be a Texas Longhorn.

From high school freshman to college freshman, Kevin had grown six inches – and he wasn't finished growing yet!

High school freshman
6 ft 2 in (1.88 m)

High school senior
6 ft 7 in (2.01 m)

College freshman
6 ft 9 in (2.06 m)

The Longhorn coaches knew they had something special in Kevin Durant. He was the full package. Kevin not only had height on his side. He could shoot with incredible accuracy, whether close to the rim or at long range, and he could move with speed and agility around the floor like a much smaller player.

In Texas, Kevin worked with a strength and conditioning coach called Todd Wright to get him ready for college basketball. He needed to add more strength and muscle to his tall and lean physique. Coach Wright helped him gain weight, strengthen the weaker parts of his body and make his tighter parts more flexible.

Kevin went on to have one of the greatest freshman years in college basketball EVER!

He scored more than 10 points in every one of his 35 games. And more than 20 points in all of his first seven games!

His highest score in a game was a whopping 37 points, which he achieved four times!

Kevin was the highest scoring freshman that year, with an average of 25.8 points. He left soon-to-be NBA superstar Steph Curry, who was a freshman at Davidson College, in second place with a point average of 21.5!

And he led the Longhorns to a 25-10 record that season, with a 15-1 record at home.

Kevin finished his freshman year with masses of accolades and accomplishments.

- Naismith Award
- Wooden Award
- Adolph Rupp Trophy
- Oscar Robertson Trophy
- Big 12 Tournament MVP
- Big 12 Player of the Year
- Big 12 Freshman of the Year

Kevin was named consensus National Player of the Year for 2007. An honour that no other freshman in the history of college basketball had achieved before!

The National Player of the Year award is composed of six separate player of the year awards. Only 30 different players have achieved all major basketball Player of the Year awards in a single season., and before Kevin they had all been more experienced college players.

Famous consensus National Player of the Year the winners include...

Michael Jordan
(college junior)
North Carolina
1984

Larry Bird
(college senior)
Indiana State
1979

Tim Duncan
(college senior)
Wake Forest
1997

Kevin opened the doors for other freshmen to win the award, including Anthony Davis (2012), Zion Williamson (2019) and Cooper Flagg (2025).

After one year at college, Kevin felt ready to take the big leap to the NBA. There's an NBA rule that all basketball players in the US must attend college for at least one year before they turn professional. This rule was made in 2005, when Kevin was still at high school. If it hadn't been, he could have joined the NBA in 2006.

Kevin has since said he would have chosen to go to the NBA in 2006 because his favourite childhood team, the Toronto Raptors, had first pick in the NBA Draft that year. But Kevin's path was to go to college – and he didn't regret it. He became much more skilled and experienced in that year.

Kevin loved the Toronto Raptors as a kid because he was a big fan of their star player Vince Carter, an amazing slam dunker. He also loved their jerseys, which at one time featured a dinosaur!

Many outstanding basketball players only go to college for one year. They're known as "one-and-done" players – and Kevin is one of them.

Other NBA one-and-doners are...

Carmelo Anthony
NBA Draft: 2003
Team: Denver Nuggets

Kevin Love
NBA Draft: 2008
Team: Minnesota Timberwolves

Some standout players that are a little older than KD didn't go to college at all, including LeBron James, Kobe Bryant and Kevin Garnett.

Even though Kevin had had one of the greatest one-and-done seasons in the history of college basketball, he was only considered the SECOND-best player in his year. Unbelievably, someone else had a year that matched or even surpassed KD's. That player was Greg Oden.

Greg was a standout freshman at Ohio State University. A 7 ft (2.13 m) tall centre, he was powerful and dominant on the court with a big personality. Many people were comparing him to some of the greatest centres, including Shaquille O'Neal and David Robertson.

Greg led his college team, the Ohio State Buckeyes, to a 35-4 record and their first national title game since 1962 in the NCAA (National Collegiate Athletic Association) Tournament – the biggest national tournament in the college basketball calendar. He was also the first freshman to win the Big Ten Defensive Player of the Year award.

Kevin, on the other hand, had missed out on NCAA Tournament glory with the Texas Longhorns. They crashed out in the second round. This loss had an impact on Kevin's impressive college stats, but there was still no doubt he was one of the best college players ever.

All eyes were on Kevin and Greg ahead of the 2007 NBA Draft and there was a lot of speculation over which one-and-doner would be picked first.

The NBA Draft is an event where professional basketball teams select players each year. There's a lottery system to decide who picks first, and in the 2007 Draft, the Portland Trail Blazers had the first pick.

And they picked Greg Oden.

But Kevin wasn't far behind him – he was picked second by the Seattle SuperSonics!

Both players were brilliant at their game, and each of them had the potential to become the best of their generation. But sadly, only one of them would fulfil their potential in the NBA.

After joining the Portland Trail Blazers, Greg missed his whole rookie season due to a knee injury. Plagued by more injuries, he played less than 100 games In the NBA before leaving the league.

Kevin didn't know much about his new team, the SuperSonics – he had expected to be picked first! But behind the scenes they were clearing the way for their new young star to shine. They were letting some players go and starting to build a new team around him.

It was the dawn of a new era for KD and, as usual, he was up to the challenge.

CHAPTER 5
NBA GIANT

Kevin was still only 19 years old in his rookie season in the NBA. He had a lot to prove and a whole team to carry when it came to scoring points. He was their lead offensive player – the only one who could shoot hoops consistently.

Kevin took a little while to find his feet in the NBA. It wasn't until the ninth game that Kevin experienced his first victory with the SuperSonics. But from there, he began to show his star potential.

In a game against the Indiana Pacers in the first half of the season, Kevin scored 35 points, making him the second-youngest player in NBA history to score more than 30 points in a game! At the time, only LeBron James was younger when he achieved the feat.

He went on to score more than 30 points four more times, but he saved the best score for last. In the final game of the season against the Golden State Warriors, Kevin hit his rookie season high of 42 points!

Kevin finished the season with averages of 20.3 points, 4.4 rebounds and 2.4 assists. He was the only rookie that season to hit a 20-point average, and he became only the third teenage player ever to achieve the feat.

Hardly any teenage NBA stars in history have averaged 20 points per game as rookies.

PLAYER	TEAM	ROOKIE SEASON
LeBron James	Cleveland Cavaliers	2003–2004
Carmelo Anthony	Denver Nuggets	2003–2004
Kevin Durant	Seattle SuperSonics	2007–2008
Luka Dončić	Dallas Mavericks	2018–2019
Zion Williamson	New Orleans Pelicans	2019–2020
Victor Wembanyama	San Antonio Spurs	2023–2024

For his outstanding efforts in his first year with the Seattle SuperSonics, Kevin was crowned 2008 NBA Rookie of the Year! He was the first player in the SuperSonics' history to win the award.

AVERAGE POINTS PER GAME

20.9

21.0

20.3

21.2

22.5

21.4

Despite KD's amazing statistics and skills, the Seattle SuperSonics were struggling as a team. They had a record of only 20 wins and 62 losses for the 2007-2008 season – the worst in the league and in the team's history. There were also legal battles over building a new arena for the team.

Something had to change... and it did in a big way. The team relocated to Oklahoma City, the hometown of owner Clay Bennett! The Seattle SuperSonics became the Oklahoma City Thunder and, just like that, Kevin was the face of a new franchise.

Thirteen years before Kevin arrived, Oklahoma City had experienced a devastating terrorist attack: the Oklahoma City bombing. A huge car bomb went off outside a government building, killing and injuring hundreds of people.

Many years later, the city was still trying to rebuild itself – and one of the things they were creating was a new NBA-level basketball arena. Kevin could immediately see how important basketball could become in Oklahoma City.

Kevin started working even harder in the gym, he ate wholesome meals and he took good care of himself. For his second season in the NBA, Kevin was determined to make Oklahoma City proud.

And he really did! Kevin gave everything to the team in his sophomore season. He led the Thunder valiantly, even if the team's record didn't improve an awful lot that year. They finished up with a slightly better but still disappointing 23–59 record. Nevertheless, their star player was still shining.

Kevin improved his points average by five points – bringing it up to 25.3. This jump put Kevin in line for the NBA's Most Improved Player Award, but he finished third in the voting. (Danny Granger of the Indiana Pacers claimed it that year.)

He also showed his massive worth in the Rising Stars Challenge at the All-Star weekend. The previous year as a rookie, Kevin had starred in the event, which is a game where the NBA's best rookies take on the best sophomores. But this time, as a sophomore, Kevin really brought his A-game.

KD led the Sophomores to victory and netted 46 points, setting a Rising Stars Challenge record! He was also voted the game MVP.

The previous Rising Stars Challenge points record had stood for five years before Kevin came along and smashed it. Amar'e Stoudemire of the Phoenix Suns set the previous record of 36 points back in 2004.

There was no denying that Kevin's star was on the rise, and the Oklahoma City Thunder were rising with him. By the end of Kevin's second season in the NBA, the team had found their groove and they were starting to look more like a team to watch. But Kevin couldn't do it all alone, and thanks to a new Thunder recruit in the 2008 draft, he didn't have to...

Russell Westbrook was a point guard who was beginning to show his star potential alongside Kevin. He was fast and high-energy with lots of confidence. He was also an efficient scorer.

With Russell on the team, Kevin could share the offensive load. Together, they were about to become one of the most powerful NBA duos of their generation.

Kevin was going into his third NBA season with more experience and confidence as a leader, and a stronger team than ever behind him. He'd also grown to 6 ft 11 (2.11 m) by this time, making him even more of a presence on the court.

He was a player in his prime, and the NBA was about to see what else KD could do.

CHAPTER 6
CHASING GREATNESS

Kevin might have won Rookie of the Year in his first season in the NBA and upped his points average and set NBA records in his second, but Kevin still had a lot to prove – and he set out to level up even more in his third.

Ahead of the season, he trained even harder in the gym to strengthen and bulk up his body, so it wasn't as lean.

The Oklahoma City Thunder were also focused on building the best team possible around Kevin that year. In the 2009 NBA Draft, they had won third pick. There were a lot of talented players in the draft, including future NBA legend Steph Curry. But the Thunder knew just who they needed: shooting guard James Harden.

Like Kevin and Russell Westbrook, James could shoot brilliantly, especially from beyond the three-point line. The Thunder needed James to space out the team on the floor. They thought he would create a powerful trio with Kevin and Russell...

...and they weren't wrong! With James Harden on board and the chemistry between KD and Russell growing, plus other awesome players like Jeff Green and Serge Ibaka in the team, the Thunder took the NBA by storm that year.

For starters, they won a lot more games than last season, finishing up with a 50-32 record. Then they surpassed all expectations by making it to the NBA play-offs! They were the youngest team ever to achieve the feat.

Could Kevin handle the pressure of the play-offs?

The play-offs are a tournament at the end of the season between the best seven sides in a conference. The winning team in the West plays the top team in the East in the NBA Finals to decide who wins the league.

BASKETBALL I.D.

NAME: Russell Westbrook

DATE OF BIRTH: 12th November 1988

POSITION: Point guard

TEAMS: Oklahoma City Thunder, Houston Rockets, Washington Wizards, Los Angeles Lakers, Los Angeles Clippers, Denver Nuggets, Sacramento Kings

YEARS IN NBA: 2008–present

RELATIONSHIP TO KEVIN: Teenage teammate

BASKETBALL I.D.

NAME: James Harden

DATE OF BIRTH: 26th August 1989

POSITION: Shooting guard

TEAMS: Oklahoma City Thunder, Houston Rockets, Brooklyn Nets, Philadelphia 76ers, Los Angeles Clippers

YEARS IN NBA: 2009–present

RELATIONSHIP TO KEVIN: Thunder teammates

It was the team's first play-offs spot since 2005, and their first-ever as the Oklahoma City Thunder. Unfortunately for them, they faced the Los Angeles Lakers in the first round of the play-offs. Led by NBA legend and one of Kevin's favourite players, Kobe Bryant, the Lakers were very tough opponents.

Things weren't looking good when the Thunder initially lost the first two games of the series, but they fought back in the next two games, bringing the scoreline to 2-2.

Always.

Kevin was not intimidated by his hero Kobe and scored a lot of points across the games, but it wasn't enough to win the series of up to seven games. The Lakers eventually triumphed, winning four games to two, and they went on to win the NBA Finals that year.

The play-offs ended in disappointment, but the Thunder had achieved a lot to get there. And across his third NBA season, Kevin had proven that he was one of the greatest players in the league.

Kevin's points average jumped up to 30.1, making him the top scorer in the NBA that year. At age 21, he became the youngest player in history to take the scoring title!

Kevin was also selected for the NBA All-Star Game at the annual All-Star weekend for the first time. The All-Star Game pits the NBA's best players in the Eastern and Western conferences against each other. Basketball fans, players and the media vote for the All-Stars each season. He became the Oklahoma City Thunder's first All-Star under their new name.

This kicked off a run of nine All-Star selections for KD. In total, he has been selected for the huge event 15 times in his career, putting him in joint fourth place for the most All-Star Game appearances in NBA history.

Only LeBron James (21 times), Kareem Abdul Jabbar (19 times) and Kobe Bryant (18 times) have been selected for the All-Star Game more than Kevin. Will KD rise further up the ranks?

Kevin was also named for the first time in the All-NBA Team, an honour given to the best players across the whole NBA. He was selected in the first team (out of three teams) alongside a roster of NBA superstars.

2009–2010 ALL-NBA FIRST TEAM	
PLAYER	TEAM
Kevin Durant	Oklahoma City Thunder
Lebron James	Cleveland Cavaliers
Dwight Howard	Orlando Magic
Kobe Bryant	Los Angeles Lakers
Dwayne Wade	Miami Heat

Kevin has since been selected for the first team five more times in his career, and a further five times for the second team.

KD got his first taste of international success in 2010, too, at the FIBA World Championships in Turkey. In his first-ever selection for Team USA, Kevin was also named as the team's leader because other, more established international players weren't available.

Kevin took his chance to show the world what he could do by leading the team to win the tournament and the gold medal! It was Team USA's first FIBA World Championship win since 1994. He was also crowned tournament MVP and the USA Male Basketball Athlete of the Year for the first time.

Kevin has won the USA Male Athlete of the Year award a record three times, in 2010, 2016 (when he shared it with Carmelo Anthony) and 2021. The award honours that year's top performer in international competitions.

At the start of his fourth season in the NBA, Kevin agreed a new, five-year contract with the Oklahoma City Thunder. He was there to stay, and he was hungry for more success.

Kevin was still only 22, but his standout Team USA performance, his strong first three seasons in the NBA, and his cool, calm demeanour meant people were really starting to see him as an elite player, including the president of the United States!

On September 18th 2010, Kevin travelled back to his hometown of Washington, D.C. to play basketball with Barack Obama at the White House. He took his teammates Eric Maynor and James Harden along too, plus his mother Wanda and grandmother Barbara.

Kevin was reaching new heights of fame and popularity. What would he achieve in his next NBA season?

The answer is A LOT! The Slim Reaper just kept getting more deadly in the 2010-2011 season.

With a points average of 27.7 per game, Kevin topped the NBA as scoring champion for the second year running.

He also led the Thunder to yet more victories, finishing the season with a 55-27 record. There were incredible performances from other key players in the Thunder lineup, too, including Russell Westbrook, who joined Kevin as an All-Star that year. His team-up with Kevin was proving magical.

The team finished in fourth place in their league, the Western Conference. After the main season ended, the play-offs began, and the Thunder looked like more of a threat than ever before.

On their play-offs journey, the Thunder first beat the Denver Nuggets in five games to make it through Round One.

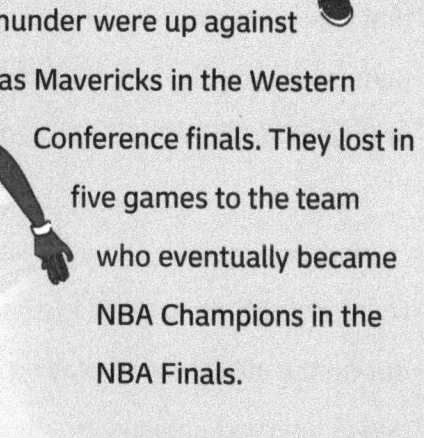

Then they faced the Memphis Grizzlies in the Western Conference semi-finals. They beat them in seven games!

The Thunder were up against the Dallas Mavericks in the Western Conference finals. They lost in five games to the team who eventually became NBA Champions in the NBA Finals.

Despite their play-offs loss, Kevin and his teammates held their heads high. The Thunder were the second-youngest team ever to make the Conference Finals. And next year, they knew they could go even further...

But their ambitions had to wait a little while because Kevin's fifth season in the NBA began with a lockout: all play stopped because of legal disagreements between team owners and the union that represented all basketball players. There were no games for months, and players couldn't train or practice together.

Nothing was going to stop Kevin getting on the court, though. He trained just as hard as he ever did during the 2011 lockout, playing in exhibition games and in international and amateur leagues.

Kevin even worked out with LeBron James, who was always seen as Kevin's biggest competition. The two giants of the game worked together to improve their play and showed the world that they were more friends than rivals.

When the 2011-2012 season did finally get started, Kevin was ready to go! He led the Thunder to win 20 out of their first 25 games. Then, in a win against the Denver Nuggets, Kevin netted 51 points, the highest score in his NBA career at that point.

That was a great game for Russell Westbrook too, who scored 40 points. His score combined with Kevin's made them one of the highest scoring duos in NBA history.

Once again, Kevin was named NBA scoring champion that season with an average of 28 points, 8 rebounds and 3.5 assists. He was the first player since Michael Jordan to win the title three seasons in a row.

KD went on to win the title one more time in 2014, bringing his total number of wins to four and shooting him up to joint third in NBA history behind legends Michael Jordan and Wilt Chamberlain. George Gerwin and Allen Iverson also won it four times.

Michael Jordan, *10-time scoring champion*

Wilt Chamberlain, *7-time scoring champion*

Kevin dominated at the All-Star Game that season, too, scoring 36 points! He was crowned All-Star MVP for the first time in his career.

The Thunder improved their season record again that year, with 47 wins and only 19 losses. They placed second in the Western Conference behind the San Antonio Spurs. Just like their superstar Kevin, the Thunder were consistently getting better and better. Would this be the year they'd make it to the NBA Finals?

Yes! They thundered through the play-offs, defeating the Dallas Mavericks – the defending NBA champions – in just four games in the first round.

Then came the Los Angeles Lakers in the Conference semi-finals. The Thunder took them out in five games.

The San Antonio Spurs fell to the Thunder in the Conference finals in six games... and at last the Thunder had their chance in the NBA Finals.

The Thunder hadn't reached the NBA Finals since 1996 – almost 20 years before that, when they were playing as the Seattle SuperSonics. In 2012, they faced a big challenge in the form of The Big Three: Miami Heat's superteam formed of LeBron James, Dwyane Wade and Chris Bosh.

The Big Three looked unstoppable, and unfortunately for Kevin and the Thunder, they were. The Thunder won the first game but lost the next four. It was not to be that time, but Kevin wasn't going to give up on his dream of winning the NBA title.

CHAPTER 7
NUMBER ONE

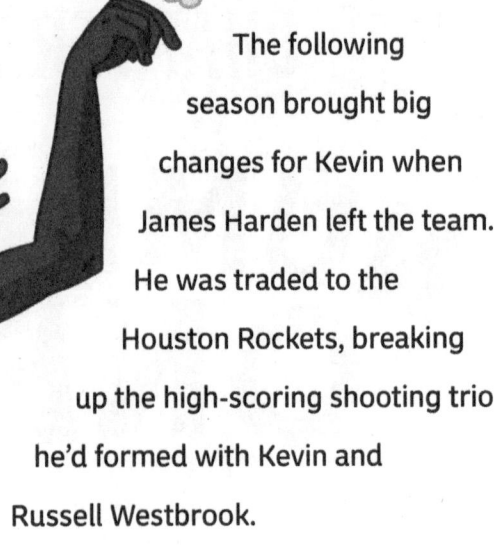

The following season brought big changes for Kevin when James Harden left the team. He was traded to the Houston Rockets, breaking up the high-scoring shooting trio he'd formed with Kevin and Russell Westbrook.

It was a blow for the team that came about because the Thunder couldn't afford to pay all three of their top players high salaries. With James gone, Kevin had to take on more shooting responsibilities. It took him a little while to find his feet in the new set-up, but once he did, he was riding high once again.

KD posted consistently high scores in the 2012–2013 season – including 52 points in one game against the Dallas Mavericks – but his average of 28.1 points wasn't quite enough to defend his NBA scoring title that year. Carmelo Anthony of the New York Knicks claimed the top spot instead.

Still, Kevin did lead the Thunder to win 60 games out of 82, placing them top of the Western Conference for the first time in Kevin's career, and second in the NBA overall.

This was also the season when Kevin joined the 50-40-90 club. The criteria for entry into this exclusive group of NBA players is to have...

AT LEAST 50% OF SHOTS FROM THE FIELD

AT LEAST 40% OF SHOTS FROM THE THREE-POINT AREA

AT LEAST 90% OF SHOTS FROM THE FREE-THROW LINE

The percentages represent the amount of goals a player actually makes out of all their attempts.

"From the field" means any shot on the court, and the three-point area is anywhere behind the three-point line. The free throw line is where players shoot if they have been fouled.

Kevin entered the NBA record books when he joined the 50-40-90 club alongside only nine other NBA players in history. When Kevin achieved the feat again in 2023, he became one of only three players – alongside Larry Bird and Steve Nash – to do it twice and the first player to achieve 55-40-90!

Despite his outstanding 50-40-90 achievement and six impressive seasons behind him, Kevin still hadn't been awarded the NBA MVP. That's the award given to the most standout player in a season, voted for by sports writers and broadcasters.

The previous year, Kevin had lost out to LeBron James, and in the 2012–2013 season, he lost to his closest rival for a second time. LeBron and Kevin were widely viewed as the two best players in the league at that time, and Kevin seemed to always finish second to The King. It was beginning to get on his nerves!

LeBron was on a winning streak, having won the NBA MVP four times since 2008. When would Kevin get his chance?

Thankfully, Kevin didn't have to wait much longer! The following season was one of his greatest.

He went on a high-scoring rampage, eventually beating Michael Jordan's NBA record for consecutive games scoring 25 points or more. MJ's record was 40 games; KD surpassed it at 41. Kevin also scored a career high of 54 points in a game against the Golden State Warriors.

He ended the season with a scoring average of 32 points per game – an Oklahoma City Thunder record that still stands today.

Wilt Chamberlain holds the record for longest high-scoring streak in NBA history. He scored 25 points or more in 80 straight games in the 1961–1962 season. Oscar Robertson had a run of 46 straight games with 25+ points in 1963–1964.

Kevin was crowned NBA MVP at last! Finally, he was number one and NOT number two, as he had seemed to be throughout his career – whether it was to Greg Oden in college and the NBA Draft, or LeBron James in the NBA.

Kevin just edged it over LeBron for MVP. LeBron was a phenomenal all-round player that year, but Kevin had really stepped up for his team when his shooting partner, Russell Westbrook, was out with a knee injury for many months. Kevin carried the entire offensive load for the Thunder, confidently leading them to second place in the Western Conference.

KD VS LBJ: 2013-2014 SEASON STATS

	KEVIN DURANT (Oklahoma City Thunder)	**LEBRON JAMES** (Miami Heat)
Average points per game	32.0	27.1
Most points per game	54	61
Average rebounds per game	7.4	6.9
Average assists per game	5.5	27.1
Total points	2,593	2,089
Team record	59–23	54–28
Team league position	2nd (Eastern)	2nd (Eastern)

When Kevin accepted his NBA MVP award on 6th May 2014, he gave a heartfelt speech that resonated with many people around the world. He first thanked everyone who had helped him along the way at the Oklahoma City Thunder, especially his teammate Russell Westbrook. Lastly, he turned to his mother, Wanda, who was in the front row of the audience.

With tears in his eyes and a wobbly voice, Kevin thanked Wanda for all she had done for him and his brother when they were young.

Those four words at the end of Kevin's emotional speech became iconic. They not only told everyone watching what a wonderful woman his mum was in the best way Kevin could, but they also showed appreciation for mothers everywhere.

Kevin's speech is still talked about more than a decade later as a special moment that was just as important as the award he was accepting.

CHAPTER 8
GOING FOR GOLD

Kevin's next NBA season was derailed by foot injuries and he only managed to play in 27 games. It was a very tough year for Kevin, and at times he wondered if he'd ever get back on form.

But Kevin stayed strong mentally and physically, and by the 2015-2016 season, he was back and starting to look like his MVP self again. His points average came back up to 28.2, with 8.2 rebounds and 5.0 assists, and the Thunder finished up third in the Western Conference with a 55-27 record.

That wasn't a bad result in a year that saw the Golden City Warriors break NBA records with 73 wins, and the San Antonio Spurs finish just behind them with 67 wins.

The Thunder faced the high-flying Golden State Warriors in the Conference Finals that year, having defeated the Dallas Mavericks and the San Antonio Spurs in the previous rounds.

Kevin notched up big scores across the seven-game series, but it eventually ended with a 4–3 loss for the Thunder.

Little did the Thunder know that they were about to concede another loss to the Golden State Warriors... their star player!

In the summer of 2016, Kevin announced that he was leaving the Oklahoma City Thunder for the Golden State Warriors. The Warriors had lost the NBA Finals the previous season, but they were major contenders for the NBA Championship.

Kevin had been loyal to the Thunder for nine years and he'd achieved so much with them, but he had never tasted NBA Finals success. The Golden State Warriors seemed like his best option for that.

But not all NBA fans were happy. They saw it as taking the easy route to winning a ring.

Each member of the winning team at the NBA Finals is given a specially designed championship ring, featuring the year, the player's name and the team name.

At the Golden State Warriors, Kevin joined three other All-Star players to form one of the greatest superteams the NBA had ever seen. Stephen Curry, Klay Thompson and Draymond Green were already established as a powerful trio for the Warriors. Adding Kevin into the mix turned them into the "Fantastic Four".

Klay Thompson
Shooting guard

Kevin Durant
Small forward

Draymond Green
Power forward

Steph Curry
Point guard

The Warriors' formidable new lineup made magic in the NBA, and together they won back-to-back NBA championships together in 2017 and 2018! Kevin could finally call himself an NBA champion after countless play-off disappointments.

2017

2018

The icing on the cake for Kevin was winning back-to-back NBA Finals MVP awards. When Kevin first won the award in 2017, he was still only in his first season with the Warriors. When he won two consecutive awards, he became one of only 12 players in NBA history to win the award more than once.

The Warriors reached the NBA Finals again in 2019 and they hoped to win a "three-peat", but it wasn't to be. The Warriors lost in six games to the Toronto Raptors. Injuries meant that Kevin had to miss many of the play-off games that year.

After huge success in his three years with the Golden State Warriors, Kevin felt it was time to move on – this time to the Brooklyn Nets. As a sign of respect for all Kevin had done for the franchise, the Warriors retired his number 35 jersey. That means no other player will wear that number for the team again.

> A retired jersey is one of the greatest honours an NBA player can receive. The jersey is usually hung from the rafters with other retired jerseys in the team's arena.

Kevin decided to wear the number 7 jersey at the Brooklyn Nets to mark a new era in his life. But this new era took a little while to get started. Kevin missed his entire first season due to injury and the coronavirus pandemic.

He was back on form for the Nets in the next two seasons, and the team built a strong line-up around Kevin, including fellow All-Star Kyrie Irving and Kevin's old friend James Harden. But championship success kept eluding them and Kevin kept picking up more injuries.

Kevin was traded to the Phoenix Suns in 2023 where he added more and more points to his NBA career scoring total. In the 2024–2025 season, Kevin reached 30,000 career points! He is only the eighth player in NBA history to do so.

There's no doubt Kevin is now an all-time great in the NBA, but he's probably THE all-time great for Team USA. No player has had more success in international basketball than Kevin.

He has played in four Olympic Games – in 2012, 2016, 2020 and 2024 – and won gold medals in all four. No other male basketball player in history has that many gold medals! He actually has five including the one he won in the 2010 FIBA World Cup.

Carmelo Anthony and LeBron James also have four medals each, but they have three gold and a bronze.

During the Paris Olympic Games in 2024, Kevin broke Team USA's all-time scoring record of 488 points, which was previously held by women's player Lisa Leslie. He's now scored 518 points for Team USA. The closest male player to that score is LeBron James with 358 points, so it might be some time before someone beats Kevin's record.

RANK	PLAYER	CAREER POINTS	POINTS AVERAGE
1	Kevin Durant	518	18.5
2	LeBron James	358	11.9
3	Carmelo Anthony	336	10.8
4	David Robertson	270	11.3
5	Michael Jordan	256	16.0

TEAM USA'S TOP MALE SCORERS

Will KD play in the 2028 Los Angeles Olympic Games? He hasn't ruled it out!

In 2025, after two strong years at the Phoenix Suns, he signed with the Houston Rockets. Now in his late 30s and heading into his 18th NBA season, Kevin is still scoring big, breaking records and working as hard as ever. Not many players have passed age 35 and played the way KD still can. But Kevin is different – and he likes it that way.

"I know that hard work got me here. And the day I stop working hard, this can all go away."

CHAPTER 9

OFF THE COURT

Kevin is a basketball machine. He spends much of his time playing and practising, or training hard at the gym to improve his performance. He lives and breathes basketball, and he's built his life around it. But who is he beyond the game?

He is still very close to his family, especially his mum Wanda. Kevin's memorable NBA MVP speech about his mum made her story famous, and a few years later the rapper, actress and film producer Queen Latifah made a movie about her life called *The Real MVP: The Wanda Durant Story*.

He has his mum's name tattooed on one side of his chest, and his grandmother's name, Barbara, on the other. Sadly, Kevin lost Barbara in 2022.

Kevin's older brother Tony is a big part of his life, too. Tony also played basketball, and is now a dad to two boys, Jadyn and Anthony Jr. They regularly support their Uncle Kevin at basketball games.

Kevin also has two younger siblings on his dad's side, Brianna and Rayvonne. They look up to their big brother and Kevin tries hard to set a good example for them. Kevin also remains very tight with his dad, Wayne Pratt, many years after they rebuilt their relationship.

Having played for teams all over the country in his 17-year NBA career, he has homes all over the US. In any downtime he has, Kevin loves playing video games!

As one of the most recognisable and popular names in the NBA, many global brands have wanted to work with Kevin over the years, including Foot Locker, Google, the video game NBA 2K and the drinks brands Gatorade and Prime.

Way back as a young rookie, Kevin signed a $60-million deal with Nike to make his own brand of shoes. It was the second-highest rookie deal in history at the time (behind LeBron's $90-million rookie deal, naturally!). Kevin has now released 18 shoes and counting in his "KD" line. Many of his KD shoes come in a pink "Aunt Pearl" colourway in honour of his beloved aunt and women's cancer charities.

Kevin not only sells shoes with Nike – he also works with the company to fund community basketball projects that make the game accessible to all. In 2023, Kevin signed a lifetime deal with Nike. Only Michael Jordan and LeBron James had received lifetime deals with Nike before Kevin.

Kevin has used his advertising and basketball earnings to found companies and establish himself as a talented businessman. Alongside his business partner Rich Kleiman, he founded a company called Thirty-Five Ventures (35V) that invests in businesses Kevin believes in, from a pickleball team and women's sports to new technologies. He also created Boardroom, a media brand that produces films and TV shows, including the drama *Swagger*, which was inspired by Kevin's life.

KD is now one of the richest NBA players in the world thanks to his big-money basketball contracts, advertising deals and business ventures. He is worth around $300 million.

But he gives back, too. Through the Durant Family Charity Foundation, Kevin funds sports facilities, educational programmes and initiatives for young people across the US and beyond.

Kevin co-founded Team Durant, an AAU basketball programme in Prince George's County, Maryland, with his dad Wayne. Kevin also opened The Durant Centre in his hometown, an educational facility for low-income students.

Kevin's charity foundation also gives to worldwide causes that are important to him, such as homelessness and social justice. In 2018, his foundation donated $1 million to the Red Cross when a tornado struck his adopted home of Oklahoma. His support encouraged the Oklahoma City Thunder and Nike to donate, too.

Kevin is a practising Christian. He sees his faith as something that keeps him humble and grounded, and it helps him overcome challenges in his life. Before he made the decision to move to the Golden State Warriors, he asked his pastor to help him decide. He has religious tattoos on his body, including the words "Walk by faith not by sight", which remind him to trust in God's plan for him.

"With everything I do, I just try to be myself."

Kevin has always stood out – at school because of his height, on the basketball court because of his accuracy and athleticism, and now on the world's stage as a successful entrepreneur and outspoken force for good. He is a shining example of what can happen when you find what you love and strive every day to do it well.

THE PLAYBOOK

All-NBA Team
An honour given to players recognised as the best in the NBA in a season. There are three teams.

All-Star
A player selected for the All-Star Game, featuring the best NBA players from each conference in a season.

assist
A pass that leads another player directly to a successful shot.

MVP
An award for the most valuable player in a game, tournament or league.

NBA
The major professional basketball league in the US.

NBA Draft
An event where teams select players who are new to the NBA.

NBA Finals
A series of up to seven games to decide the NBA champions each year.

NBA Play-offs
An annual tournament for the top eight in each conference (after the regular season).

turnover
When a player loses the ball to another player.

Western/Eastern conference
The two leagues of the NBA. They both contain 15 teams.

ABOUT THE AUTHORS

Hannah has been creating children's books for most of her adult life. After studying English, she worked for a big publisher, making books about stuff like LEGO, Star Wars, Disney movies, computer games and comics. Now she works for herself, still making all kinds of fun books, like this one! She loves playing sports, cooking, and hanging out with her two kids.

Carl's first illustrated book was released the day he graduated from university. He has worked for many publishers, drawing upon his childhood love of Spielberg movies, comic books and Saturday morning cartoons. Carl lives in the hills of North Wales overlooking the sea, with his wife Ceri and their two children who are also budding mini illustrators.